Inspirational Values

Finding Y

CW01499177

DISCOVERING WHO YOU ARE, REMAINING TRUE TO
YOURSELF, STRIVING TOWARDS BECOMING ROLE
MODELS TO FAMILY AND FRIENDS. IMPROVE
IMPERFECTIONS AND EMBRACE STRENGTH, PEACE, LOVE
AND HAPPINESS.

Doreen Esijemine Aderonke Omaghomi

Dafour Design Concepts Ltd

ISBN: 978-1-915889-84-3

DEDICATED TO MY DAUGHTER

MONICA TORI ALERO OLAITAN OJEWALE

CONTENTS

PREFACE

From my heart to all you lovely special people out there who have no one to talk to, no one to cry out to, nobody with whom to share joy and misery; our young children, youth and even some adults in various walks of life who are in unfortunate dire positions for survival. Life in general can get complicated with children, teenagers or even some grown-ups. Sometimes life has a way of dealing its cards. For instance, having to become separated from parents at the very tender age of seven or eight to go and live with relatives, especially if the parents find it a struggle to feed their large family, or for some other reason. This is predominantly an African attribute, purposely to give the child/children the best quality of life. The problem is some of these maternal or paternal uncles or aunties may have little or no time for their nephews or nieces who will at some point need their attention; instead, they are laden with chores without help, while their own offspring loiter around doing absolutely *zilch*. The irony of it all is that in the long run, the less privileged are those who are likely to benefit from any kind of mal-treatment because it toughens them up; don't get me wrong, there will be tears from time to time, but behind those tears lies the determination to become somebody in life, to make their parents proud; to potentially change the world through love.

There is one important inappropriate habit we should try not to entertain…to hastily condemn any unruly child/children, because unbeknown to the whole world is what goes on behind closed doors. There are families out there who do not experience major undesirable phases with any of their children, while quite a number of parents go through phases of difficult times with theirs. Parents who are lucky enough to sail through with their children undisturbed should not judge those parents as incompetent; rather, we can offer support by praying for them, for God to grant them the gift of love, humility, peace and togetherness. Remember, challenges come in different forms. Children are gifts from God and it is the duty of parents to nurture, support and guide them aright, with the help of God through prayers. In my opinion, being prayerful and close to God is a way of finding peace. It has helped me become the person I am today. The bearer of inner peace is someone in a better position to enlighten you, through experiences of God's glory. Our heavenly father loves us all. He created us; He knows our individual potential. Though there will be difficult times, He will never give each one of us more than our share to bear. When, not if, you find yourself in sticky situations, accept them as lessons or part of life's experiences. Life is all about learning; through determination and consistency we become stronger in the process of fulfilling our dreams.

As mentioned earlier, I am a mother to a daughter and it was this relationship that inspired me to put pen to paper. My expectations of a man, especially fathers who read this book are to draw closer to their children especially their daughters, to refrain from holding back on their experiences with women and guide them step by step when they reach the appropriate age for relationships in the young love department, to teach them what to look out for and how to protect themselves in public.

To all my readers, I am not a professional in this area. These are my experiences and reflections from my time as a parent.

READ ON

Prayer! We must resort to a prayerful life. The scripture says, pray without ceasing. What that means is, no matter how dejected or put off, or how angry you are because you feel God is not listening, NEVER STOP PRAYING. What we do not realise is when we cease in prayer, we become idle in our spiritual life and that leaves room for all sorts of destructive erroneous opinions. Most times when we are preparing to pray we get distracted. There is that loud voice relentlessly trying to sway us. *You're missing out, don't bother! Remember the ginger cake topped with toffee sauce in the kitchen? Go get some and relax with your favourite programme coming up in five minutes.* That voice is always there to distract us, because it knows we are about to receive our blessings for the day and can unleash a more powerful weapon on our enemies through the Holy Spirit. Whenever you find yourself being teased or tested, rebuke it by calling the name JESUS – Even just making the sign of the cross will relieve you of any binding force. That is the habit we need to develop to free ourselves – Prayer and faith can see us through life if only we know how to apply them. Ask God for what you desire and while at it, pray for the grace for a listening ear and how to convert and implement messages. Until we begin to understand, reflect and genuinely abide by the word of God, we will remain in darkness. We need the light to flourish. Pray from your heart and mean what you say, for only then will God begin to pay attention because then you would have proven to Him you know what you want or need – I learnt that in due time; it is like a short cut to a long route. If you are not the prayerful type and you want to be close to God, you can start by asking Him to teach you how to be humble. *There's a start!* As a beginner, speak to God freely from your heart. With time perfection will prevail. Think about the words we say. Creating a scenario in our minds and following it like a story will help. For example, when you say the Lord's Prayer, close your eyes and visualise God sitting on a throne, with His arms stretched out towards you, as if to say, *yes my child, I am listening.* God will listen to you, only when you are sure of what you ask and you are ready to embrace it. So you see my dear people, God does hear us when we pray, but we often conclude He turns a deaf ear when there is little or no improvement in whatever ill circumstances lurking. The reason for this could be that His will must take precedence over the desires of our hearts, possibly because He has a mission for each one of us; for example, the deprived children earlier mentioned (who are hopefully now mature adults) had to go through that experience as children for future purposes, to learn how to treat people fairly, which in turn could significantly over time have a positive impact on people who took advantage of others. Another reason we feel God does not hear us could be that we are not fervently prayerful to make that contact or feel that overwhelming connection. A possible way of making that connection with God is to be at peace with ourselves and be true to ourselves; in that way we allow the Holy Spirit elevate us as we relinquish grudges borne against anyone and set our minds free to receive messages from above. One is better off doing what is needed at the present time rather than later. As the saying goes, *"There is no time like the present"*.

SENSITIVITY AND PURPOSE

Children seem to live on their own enclosed perfect innocent planet. Though most are sensitive, smart at times and aware of their surroundings, they occasionally come across as lost when they stare straight at you with blank eyes while we try to communicate at a level beyond their understanding. Children or teenagers may not be on the same wavelength with their parents when it comes to scolding. Please refrain from doing this in the presence of guests or relatives. It could become unpleasant and irritating when some ignorant aunties or uncles feel the need to nose in because as far as they are concerned, the parents are not strict enough with their children – all that unnecessary interfering annoying speech, going in one ear and coming out the other. I totally relate to that. Parents on the other hand know that the apple does not fall far from the tree – similarity between parents and children. In other words, personality traits good or worrying are inherited. Be patient with your children; you were once a child. It will help both parties, especially you the parent, understand your children better if you keep a record of unusual activities and also look out for personality traits. Some teenagers go through challenging phases. They could get mixed up with the wrong group, misled by the wrong type of friends or parents, erroneous opinions, become withdrawn due to bullying or it could even be an instantaneous development of a nonchalant attitude towards keeping Sunday the day of obligation holy. In this case, we can only pray to God for His guidance back to the harbour of truth and unity of faith, rather than react inappropriately which could worsen the issue.

As a Christian family, you can only but remain persistent in your duty to present your children before the Lord; pray for His grace upon your children and leave the rest to Him. Make time for heart-to-heart conversations, be it in the kitchen, bedroom, or wherever feels natural at the time. Share childhood or other useful experiences without holding back; it could help them to understand better and also realise there have been other people who have experienced and are even still encountering the same or similar quandary. Your children will love, respect and appreciate you more as that one person who is non-judgemental. Parents should neither expect perfection from their child, because it does not exist, nor condemn using profanity, but should be able to tolerate and give advice when necessary. A close bond between parent and child is paramount as it more often results in trust and loyalty. Whatever matter or situation at hand, the child will have no cause to hesitate in confiding in the parent. Correspondingly, any intrusion from *busybodies* will neither convince the parent otherwise nor obliterate any profound bond if someone tried to fabricate or concoct a story. Trust does get eroded and can take quite a long time to build back up. There is a possibility of this happening if the relationship between parents and children or husband and wife begin to lack essential qualities or if unforeseen attitudes start to encroach.

One of the advantages of being in a good marriage or relationship is the ability to trust, support and unfold the best in each other.

Some women are like *goodie bags*…not only are they virtuous, but they are also gifted. They come with enormous amounts of blessings that rub off on the husband and children. Men who are lucky enough to marry such women have to be careful not to destroy their marital homes. My neighbour, Michael, has been married to Andrea for seven years now. I have been good friends with them for a few years too because Andrea and I met through another friend. Before Michael got married, he was without a stable job and staying with his brother, Matthew. It was always one problem or the other. He eventually managed to secure and hold down a job for longer than usual. Now, Andrea on the other hand had a degree in marketing, but chose to work as a dinner lady in a very good school. They got married in June 2012. Things were going so well: contracts for Michael, children, so much laughter in their home that his colleagues wished to be as lucky. Michael treated his wife with so much love and respect because he appreciated the peace, joy, laughter and contentment that filled his home. He said he was the luckiest man ever, considering all his trials and tribulations before marriage. To date, they remain a very happy family.

Ladies, as Denzel Washington said, "A wise woman knows the importance of speaking life into her man. If you love him, believe in him, encourage him and be his peace". Ladies, endurance will make you stand out from the rest. Hmm…easier said than done, but remember that is the key. No relationship is a walk down the garden path. Be wise.

Some people are interested in what life holds in store for them; in other words, what their purpose is in life. For some it falls into place, but for others it could take a while to discover. What you enjoy doing, as in hobbies, interests, talents, present the right path or a hint to what your destiny is in life, regardless of what that interest might be. When I was in secondary school I did a lot of still life drawing and loved writing, designing and framing poems. In those days, most parents thought it was a waste of time drawing. Little did I know then it would come in handy today. There is always a reason for the talent with which you have been blessed, because sooner or later it will play a part in your life.

You should never be ashamed of your interests or goals. Talents are individually apportioned for a reason. Everyone's destiny is different. We go job-hunting or become self-employed in order to survive and even become so adept in our jobs, but there is still that passionate interest, that dream, that keeps us alive. We all have that passion for what we love doing within us that keeps us truly happy; hold onto it and never let go. If there is anything beneficial you want to do, anything at all that comes from your heart, do it. We all want the best things in life; we set goals, we dream big. Never under estimate YOU; give yourself a chance.

It is normal when fear kicks in from time to time; you are not alone there. If you fail at the first attempt try another approach. Talk to and seek advice from positive-minded people. You might get turned away if the need to approach anyone for any form of help arises, but do not dismay, do not give up; keep going no matter how little you put in on a daily basis. Carry on with goals in mind. When someone says "no" to you, whatever assistance it was you needed was not meant to happen through that person. One piece of advice people; *do not hold it against them.*

Any struggle without goals will be meaningless. *What are you pursuing; what are you trying to achieve?* Let those questions be the driving force to guide you. See, when you finally get there, those same people who turned you away, will be the same people who will want to associate with you. We inevitably encounter crunches; hard knocks do happen or else there will be no stories to tell. So when you go through hardship *finding yourself,* smile through it all because in your heart you know you are on the right path; you are focused doing the right thing, getting there inch by inch and there is a place in your heart that reminds you of that light at the end of the tunnel for which you aim. You may not know it now, but when you're older and more relaxed you will have a broader smile as you reminisce about your struggles. You will feel on top of the world with pride as you look around, what you see are most people your age who are not on the same level as yourself, yet you all started off from the same position in school. Another thing you should keep in mind is that starting off and then arriving accomplished at the same time as others is not always the case. It's like being in a classroom learning algebra; everyone in my class came to an understanding of the topic at different times, but we all got there eventually. *Algebra was one of my favourites!* On a more serious note, to achieve your goals there must be discipline and some form of consistency.

It is true that transferable skills come in handy. Some people go to university to study and graduate with a degree or two but still feel dissatisfied. That goes to show that higher educational institutions are not for everyone; we do not need to strive unnecessarily, my dearies. If that is the case, then everyone should be doctors, lawyers, architects, designers – and not road cleaners, truck drivers, bin men, shopkeepers; no one doing odd jobs. The reason we strive for success is to live happily. Work to live and don't live to work. For the fact that someone is successful in one field of work should not necessarily mean one must hastily jump onto that bandwagon. We must try not to inadvertently fall victim to greed or ignorance. We all have our individual learning styles which, if understood properly, will help us become more effective in all we do. You could be an activist, theorist, pragmatist or a reflector. Study the characteristics of each using a questionnaire to determine your style (www.skillsyouneed.com). I am a reflector; I don't normally accept the first thing that comes to mind, nor rush into making big decisions. I usually take my time, explore all pros and cons, seek advice, ask questions, ponder then eventually come up with the best solution through strong gut feelings. When I am dressing up for a night out with friends, I give myself ample time to try various outfits. After going through a number of them I don't conclude until I feel stylish and confident. I am my own person. What's your style?

When you pray to God for direction and you are granted your desire, do not hesitate to push for success. Our lives can be a lot less stressful if we take time out to figure out who we truly are and what we want; we need to find our individual paths and to have self-belief before embarking. We need to believe that each and everyone's destiny is different. You start off on the same level with your peers, but along the way you separate. Some people decide to boost their resources, while some remain in the same position...their decision. Make your life colourful and interesting by embracing and enhancing what God has given you, when you finally find YOU.

My dear people! When you need to go outside of your comfort zone, do it with care. You can think outside the box, but remember it is ok to fail. When you fail, do not be discouraged; take it as a learning curve. When you are on track towards building your future, you will get that reassurance through prayer. Each time you kneel to pray, that great feeling of contentment will engulf you because you believe and trust God; you are ready and raring to go.

Lest I forget, having a back-up plan is a great way of staying sane. What I mean by this is while you are in the moment embarking on that passion, pushing yourself, doing everything possible to see your dream become a reality, ask yourself this question – *What else can I do if this plan/project falls through, or if there is an interruption?* Believe me, this has sent enough people over the edge. It is a known fact that numerous people forget to protect their sanity. If it all falls by the wayside after the exhaustion from hard work, money spent or sleepless nights, one could potentially lose it completely. For instance, your dream is to own a Nigerian Single Dish Restaurant in the heart of town offering seasonal services. A winter dish would be fish pepper soup and assorted meat pepper soup for some heat, while in summer customers would have a choice between specially prepared beans served with fried plantain topped with stir fried sauce or with fried yam and same sauce. Location has been sorted, negotiations all in place. You have a deadline and the grand opening is drawing near. Invitations sent out to guests and all that's left to do is the installing of kitchen equipment by a very close friend who convincingly took responsibility as a favour to you. Then disaster strikes! Your friend calls to explain his predicament. You empathise but deep down, uncertainties were lurking around the edge of your subconscious regarding his part. You give a sigh of relief and hastily get on the phone to your reserve…You have a back-up plan. This is a good example of relieving yourself of insanity. There is a thin line between sanity and insanity. So my dear friends, take time to breathe, it is indispensable.

People often believe opportunities come once in a lifetime. *If that were the case, why are there second chances?* I always asked myself that question. As stated earlier, we should not forcefully develop a passion for what we never set out to achieve in the first place, believing it is an opportunity to latch on...derailing off track. This is not the same as having a back-up plan. A back-up plan is one that is originally on your to-do list that you can fall back on for the sake of sanity. Meanwhile, God has mapped out our individual opportunities. We just need to listen for the right time to push for success. It is only when that opportunity surfaces and we ignore or do not act, even with a strong gut feeling, that statement can stand...my opinion.

Why worry when you believe God is on your side? Why worry when you believe in destiny? If it is any consolation, trust in God. When I was still a nine-year-old, I once heard a man exclaim. *Why worry!* I did not understand what he meant or why he said it. He blurted it out from nowhere. We are often oblivious to other people's thoughts and worries. Their state of mind becomes meaningless to others, but to them it is perfectly clear.

Obstacles or hurdles are challenges we inevitably encounter. Never feel you are on your own. God says we should carry our crosses and follow him. These crosses are in the form of daily trials and tribulations such as problems at work, school or university assignments, people getting on your nerves, buses or trains running late, hyper-active children, anything that frustrates you. These are all challenges we face. Rather than react negatively or become despondent, the best way to handle it is to remind ourselves consciously that God carried the heavier cross, therefore a moment of adversity is only a trial, for which we should be prepared. Accepting to carry your cross willingly will always be rewarded. God has numerous ways of fulfilling His promise. He rewards us for our every effort. Whenever we plan to carry out a task but we're not sure where or how to begin and all of a sudden things fall into place, that is no coincidence; it is God rewarding you because you have done something pleasing. As the former First Lady Michelle Obama said, "You should never view your challenges as a disadvantage; instead, it is important for you to understand that your adversity is actually one of your biggest advantages. I know that because I have seen it myself, not just as a student, but years later before I came to the White House. I worked as a Dean in Colleges and in that role I encountered students who had every advantage. Their parents paid their full tuition, they lived in beautiful campus dormitories, had every material a college kid would desire: cars, computers, spending money. But when some of them got their first bad grade, they just fell apart. They lost it because they were ill-equipped to handle their first encounter with disappointment or falling short. Life will present you with many obstacles that are far worse than a bad grade, unreasonable bosses, difficult clients or patients, illnesses, losses, crises and setbacks from nowhere that will knock you off your feet. But unlike so many other young people, you will have already developed that resilience and maturity needed to carry on, even through the pain. Please, always do your part to help others".

When my daughter reached the age where she could work before going off to university, we both went round various stores to drop off her CV, while some were sent electronically. She made it clear from the outset her preferred stores which did not include the common ones; a different strategy. She wasn't prepared to lower her standards for the sake of gaining a temporary random position. Anyway, we waited for weeks without any response. She was eventually honoured with her first choice: voluntary work in a well-known government-funded medical and health care organisation in London, which she believed would set her up for future positions in the same establishment without having to apply from scratch while studying. I got regular positive feedback from the consultant who happened to be her boss.

What I am trying to portray here is that, although my daughter would have preferred a paid job, she thought of using a different strategy outside of what most teenagers her age would have done. She trusted her instincts and her parents for any constructive advice. We didn't need to convince her any further as she was doing the right thing. I told her she was starting off another phase in life and that any experience at this stage would be more beneficial than a random paid job. Voluntary work, when approached in the same manner as a paid job whole-heartedly, employers will recognise every effort and for that reason will be more inclined to put together a very good reference. This does make people stand out from the rest, but a typical teenager would not think twice before turning down non-paid work. My daughter's strategy and patience paid off. She benefited from starting off voluntarily and established herself to work in any department as an administrator in the same organisation with pay once or twice a week, or even full time. That ball was in her court!

ULTIMATE PROTECTION

Parents, please, do not get into the habit of leaving your daughters alone with a male friend or relative...regardless! It is better to be safe than sorry. These incidents do happen, where you have an uncle take advantage of a vulnerable innocent young niece, who will later be accused by other relatives of a deliberate act of consenting to incest and for not disclosing such immorality to anyone in the first place. This similar episode has been aired on one of the national British television dramas. The victim could not tell anyone, for fear of being disregarded or dismissed. So, *me no care if he ya cousin.* Daughters should be given your utmost attention in terms of protection from the so-called human lions out there that prey on the innocent and vulnerable. Growing up, I personally knew some girls in their twenties who willingly gave in to married men for the sake of money out of desperation. Parents, if you are wealthy enough, or if you are somehow comfortable financially, lavish your kids with enough money. Let them have as much as they want...as long as it is within reason. When they have enough, or know full well that their parents will always provide, all that flaunting and enticing from those animals will be to no avail; they will never fall victim to their immoral acts as long as the child is not greedy. I bet you these are the same men who will be prepared to slaughter any man who dares lay a finger on their own daughters, forgetting that what goes around does definitely come back around.

Now Daddies, you should be your daughters' best friend. You are in a better position to provide an insight into a man's world. Enlighten them; sit them down in a comfortable environment. Reveal all the dos and don'ts, the wrongs and rights, the likes and dislikes. Our girls will be safer in their environment if they are apprised of potential maltreatment or abuse from strangers or family members. Be that person in who they can confide, the one who they can turn to if conflict ensues.

Boys! My proposition for you...Love your mothers, protect your sisters and respect any lady you encounter. I had a friend who in a conversation reiterated the saying, *"The way to a man's heart is through the stomach"*. In effect, a similar saying should apply to the female species too, *"The way to a woman's heart is through affection, attention, nodding and saying 'yes dear' to everything..."* Yes, everything; *laugh out loud*. It isn't all about luxury or professing love, it's the thought behind it. You have to show it. I am always in resonance with my secondary school motto, *"ACTION NOT WORDS"* therefore, I believe action speaks louder than words. Before she returns from work, do the chores you can to lessen the task, cook something and run the bath ready for when she returns home. If you do this and other thoughtful things more often, you win a woman over a million times. I often pick the brains of my colleagues, especially the married ones. I would like to think I have a good relationship with my colleagues. We usually engage in various topics in the mess room that sometimes carry on for ages. Whenever we touch on relationship matters, I am always all ears. It was Mark's turn to enlighten us this fateful day. He told us that the secret to his marriage was to nod and agree with the missus for peace to reign: *"Oh, yes dear, you are right"*. On a more serious note, Mark spoke positively about his wife. They have been together for over thirty years. He confirmed the two main ingredients in a relationship were trust and respect, while other essentials automatically fell into place. Another colleague, Tevin, could not wait to contribute his own strategy. He met his wife Jasmine at a very young age. If it wasn't the kitchen today, it was the living room that needed upgrading – new décor, furniture, floor boards, kitchen worktop, walls, colour or even the doorbell. Tevin never hesitated to do any of that. Whatever made Jasmine happy.

Imbumba Yamadoda, an inspirational blogger from South Africa, believes in proper upbringing, especially for girls. He suggested that men have something to contribute to society in the midst of these societal changes by women. He further suggested that men should be the pillars of their own homes and if men were the head, then women were the neck; and the children the next generation. He further said that men seemed to be totally unprepared for the quality of changes women were making. For that reason, men should love their women; do not abuse them but rather pamper them. Most importantly, he said, love your girls; they will not remain under your roof as offspring forever. Each one of them belongs to a man out there who would take them as wives. Referring to men he said, *"After I have prepared my daughters to become good citizens for you as wives, your parents are preparing you to become good husbands to my girls. I want every man out there to be responsible, kind and good to others".*

I'm sure I'll be right in saying that Mr Yamadoda's suggestion resonates with us all, especially as we want our children to lead a peaceful and God-fearing life.

Ladies, same applies to us too. We know how it works for us; our own contribution to making a relationship work is equally vital. Study your man and know what makes him tick. Resolve any issue before going to bed. You know what I mean ladies. Even our men in our families, we help them grow by portraying the qualities of a good woman. So, let's put our backs into it.

LENDING A HAND

Helping people is another way of receiving favours from God. If you render help to anyone in any capacity, it is not wise to go around sounding your own trumpet to the whole world. By doing that you'll be missing out on the greatest part, which is God's own reward. Keep it to yourself. You'll be amazed at the number of unexpected favours that will come pouring your way, especially in times of hardship. Humble yourself before people. There will come a time when you will touch the lives of others on a vast scale. You don't have to be extremely wealthy to assist others, but when God blesses you or you have the added bonus of being an affluent individual, please extend the hand a little further. In honour of my dad who passed away in 2007, I decided to help those in my village improve their standard of living as a philanthropist. The plan was to operate under the radar; that was, to get well involved physically without revealing my identity. I am a logical person, so I preferred that strategy. It has always been one of my goals since secondary school to help those who are genuinely in need. The area I grew up had influenced this. There were kids my age who were very intelligent, but didn't have enough resources to keep up with their peers in terms of learning materials, uniforms, contributions towards school trips etc. Their parents were not well off, so they had to make do with what was available. This was such an impediment that it became so disheartening each time they had to purchase materials needed for a school project, or anything concerning money. Now, let's call to mind the saying that goes, *"Charity begins at home"*. It is a known fact that you are better off showing love to those nearest to you, before extending it to others. It would be pleasing to know that I would be giving a child a chance for a better life, hence my decision to extend a hand to those in my village. Offering a helping hand to those who desperately need it will forever remain in their hearts, and guess what...that will be a part of your LEGACY.

It was broadcast that a man was invited to a TV show. He was sitting with the audience, but had no clue why everyone stood up while he was asked to remain seated. He had kept a secret for fifty years, but that secret was finally uncovered. In 1938 Sir Nicholas Winton single-handedly began rescuing Jewish children from the Holocaust. He successfully brought 669 Jewish children from Czechoslovakia to Britain and helped them find new families. Most of the children's parents perished in the Auschwitz concentration camp. Winton never mentioned the children to anyone until his wife, Grete, found a notebook in the attic fifty years later. It included names and pictures of all the children that Winton had saved. His wife gave the book to a journalist and he was invited to a television program, but was oblivious to the fact that every single person in the audience was a child he had rescued. As adults now, they all came to thank him personally. Sir N W died in 2015, at the age of 106 (Newsner).

It is good practice to help your parents willingly no matter how minute. You could organise yourself by having a set time to carry out chores before going about your business for the day. You could sort out their meals, tidy up, ensure their favourite food and drink and other essentials are available on a weekly or monthly basis, however it suits you. Doing all these and more without being asked would be a wonderful blessing, because your own children or any child out there could most likely do the same and more for you. It would make them feel at peace to know that they've done something right, that the spirit of God lives in you and will continue to pray for you.

There have been some people who touched my heart with their exceptional ways of offering assistance. These were sponsors who did not own millions, yet were in the midst of all the physical operations without revealing their true identity. Helpless people in the streets could do with our help however we could, even if it were to offer a take-away meal. If you would like to assist with feeding the homeless during any festive season in your community, get in touch with your local council for all necessary procedures.

Sometimes we unexpectedly encounter so called difficult decisions. I say *so called* because we are always at liberty to make choices. It is up to us to make the right ones. We either allow our humble side prevail or we surrender to our weakness and then regret it later. It was about 1pm on a Christmas afternoon when I got a call from a friend called Tanya who lived four miles away. A few days earlier we had made plans to meet for 3pm and had a selection of meals and drinks for the day. It made sense to call at hers first, then to another friend, Esther, who lived only five minutes from me. I thought it best that way so I wouldn't have to drive too far when it got dark. All my friends call me D. Tanya asked, *"D, can you come over now pleas? I have my friend and her two kids with me. Her nine-year-old son's having toothache and was unable to sleep through the night. Could you take us to the dentist please?"* Eyes wide open, I screamed to myself, "Excuse me! On Christmas Day!" But on second thoughts I felt sympathetic towards the poor little boy. After all, there was no public transport on Christmas Day and she didn't have a car. *"I'll be there shortly"* I blurted out. *"Oh thanks D God bless"* she said. The little boy received treatment as soon as we arrived at the dentist. Happy days! I embarked on a forty-five minute drive to drop Tanya's friend and the kids off at their uncle's. I dropped Tanya off home before making my way back to mine to prepare to go to Esther's nearby. The day never went as planned with her and that was how I spent my first half of Christmas. I couldn't do much as I was tired from three masses earlier, including a vigil within two days. All along while driving them around, I did it with joy in my heart, because I knew it was what God wanted; it was my calling for the day, it was my cross to bear. I was happy still. So you see, my dear friends: it isn't the reward from people that matters, but the one from God. Sometimes our plans don't go accordingly. It might be you one day, so give a bit of love. When it happens, smile through it and be hopeful, because there is always a reason behind the unexpected.

Thank you! Those two magical words make you feel appreciated. I am sure you must have experienced an instance where you helped someone and it felt good hearing those words. It encourages you to do more. In my job in London, I have received employee recognition awards for coordinating a local programme called "valuing time" and for carrying out a safety critical job by removing a destructible item from the track, which would have caused extensive delays to the service. Management was genuinely appreciative for saving the situation and that made my day. Sometimes we don't get recognised for working hard, be it at home or at work. But never mind that because one day when least expect it, the biggest award will be presented to you; your challenge will be keeping up the good work.

My daughter is amazing when it comes to lending a hand to the homeless; she feels bad seeing people suffer, especially in the cold. There used to be a homeless man by our local superstore who she gave five pounds to every week. Put aside the fact that she is my daughter, that astounding act of humility from a teenager always urged me to pray for her continually, to always be that humble and kind-hearted individual. God bless her. I know there are many other kids like her out there. Please keep up the good nature; your rewards shall be enormous. It pleases God when we carry out corporate works of mercy.

CONFLICT & TRUST

Retaliation is for weak, opinionated, unreasonable, ignorant people. I know you are definitely not that person. It is for those who are unable to make their own honest decisions; those who are easily influenced by other losers. It is for those who have given up on progress, lost focus and are therefore out to drive you up the wall, ready to drag you down along with them. After all is said and done it doesn't need to be so. If they have chosen that path, you need to rise above that and prove to them and to yourself that you are far better than that; you are a child of God who can overcome any cowardly act. The Holy Spirit is that which controls us to act appropriately. Whenever you find yourself in an unfavourable situation, you are instantly overcome by the Holy Spirit because you believe. You allow yourself to be consumed for the sake of peace and this makes you humble and loyal not only to yourself, but to those around you. There could be people who might misconstrue your actions for weakness, but never mind that, you would be more at peace with no regrets. It is like studying to pass an exam. If you were aware of the fact that without studying hard there could be little or no chance of acquiring the best grades, you would put your back into it. If anyone decides not to study, then they would have to face the consequences when the time comes. They would have to account for their failure. Do not fall into that category of failures.

Initiating the first move to resolve a conflict between you and a friend or family member would make you the bigger person. God rewards a generous heart. If you have been offended, do not feel the need to retaliate; let it go. Your reward will be amazingly favourable at a time most needed. You will be lifting a whole lot of weight off you. Those three words *I am sorry,* almost instantly does the trick. If you ever find yourself caught between two friends and have to act as the intermediary to smooth over disagreements, it will be wise to have a think first of what to say to each person. This makes it easier to show there are no biases. A diplomatic tactic wouldn't go amiss; speak to each party separately without mentioning anything said that can infuriate the other. Both parties are bound to complain bitterly and say things that would offend the other even more, if communicated word for word. I would rather resolve issues with my partner/husband privately, than have a friend intervene. I have heard and even witnessed one occasion where a male friend took a third-party role, all in the name of helping to resolve whatever issue, but ended up getting married to the woman. He was meant to be the man's best friend. *Life, eh!*

Similarly, the world is full of people with distinctive mental and moral qualities. In life, circumstances change. There are friends and even family members who would not want you to progress, but would prefer you remained stagnant like them. Be careful with whom you share your dreams. There are some friends, relatives or even jealous partners who would try and discourage you from pursuing your goal. A partner who deems it fit to discourage you from following your dreams should be kicked to the curb, but one who encourages and supports you has your best interest at heart and will be your friend forever. You'll be surprised to know that there are *some partners* with a perverse sense of power who feel they should not be dominated. They need to wake up and smell the *"ukodo"* (Midwestern Nigerian delicacy). There was an incident that happened between a husband and a wife who had three children together. The man set his mother-in-law on his wife out of jealousy, because she refused to share the profits of her inheritance, asking her to be summoned. He even went as far as interfering with a major life-changing project, just to hurt her. Still, no man or woman in their right senses should be that spiteful. He never considered any disruptive impact on the children at all.

Trust is essential in any kind of relationship. Some people are more lenient than others when it comes to forgiving. We are all human and sometimes, yes it can be difficult to forgive and forget. Picture this! You relocate to the UK from South Africa and, prior that, you'd already made arrangements to stay with your aunt until you were settled. Among other things, she helps save your wages in one of her free accounts, until you acquire all requirements to secure yours. After about three months, she asks you to loan her some money to pay back the following week, which you do willingly. Four weeks later, she asks for same amount again, without paying back the first amount lent. This borrowing carries on for a while, which isn't fair. *What is she doing with her own salary?* you wonder. You're excited you've been offered a council flat. You visualise all the nice things with which to furnish the

27

place, and you ask for your money, only for her to retort back accusing you of being ungrateful. Seriously! *But I have been making my own contribution towards utility bills and other household items*, you say to yourself. Fear kicks in; what do you do? She is indirectly telling you to forget about your five thousand pounds. Now, this is meant to be your mum's sister. *Wonders!*

There is a tendency to fall victim to negative minded people who would be prepared to discourage you, especially if you are not strong-willed; beware of dream killers. So pick your crowd carefully, because the levels or calibres of friends you keep rub off on you. In my secondary school days the term we used for those people was NFA, meaning No Future Ambition. You do not want to get caught up in that group. Successful people do not give negative minded ones the time of day, not because they don't want to help, but for the simple fact that they lack interest and belief. Don't get confused with constructive criticism and outright discouragement. People who are not productive can never give you the right advice; neither can inexperienced people contribute positively to a particular matter. Take control of your time in life, make a distinctive choice among your calibre of friends and spend time wisely and with those who are going places. Take them seriously. You don't only learn like an apprentice; you could also become an expert in that field. So boys and girls take excellence as an attitude.

As a family, respect should exist between parents and offspring. Some parents are still stuck living in the 19th century, where children could never look their parents in the eye when reprimanded for poor behaviour...*It was hands behind you and head down, regardless of your age;* a sign of respect that still exists in some African countries. For instance, if we feel the need to remain conversant with modern technology for the sake of being part of the human race, the same concept should be applied to creating measures for free will with some element of respect within the family. Listen to your children; do not push them away. The worst thing we as parents could do is become unamiable towards our offspring. I can tell you, there are some children who would not think twice about your maternal or paternal feelings. They will walk out that door and leave you in the dark; you the parent will be left pondering where they are and in whose company. Some kids are so principled that if the parent was in the wrong, no amount of oppression from the latter would suppress the child's assertion...I have witnessed this happen between father and daughter...*I rest my case.* In this day and age, children grow up fast. Modern technology plays a massive part in enhancing their skills, almost like they were born with an embedded manual. Like it or lump it, our children are ten steps ahead of us in the gadget and social media department. My colleague Elizabeth went over to her friend Mary to collect an item brought from abroad. While discussing they were struggling to hear one another because the television was so loud. Mary had to ask her twelve-year-old daughter Olivia to reduce the volume of the television; she couldn't understand the colourful buttons on the remote control. So, if we sometimes find ourselves approaching them for help, then that should tell us that we as parents don't know it all. We live in their world now; *well to some extent.* Peace prevails in households when respect is reciprocated. On a more serious note, take time out of your busy schedule to listen to your children. It is paramount they know you can be trusted well enough to open up to you whenever and wherever.

PERSONALITY

You do not have to change your personality to suit or win people over. Be your decent self in any situation even when you're in a relationship. Develop your own style sensibly and never be ashamed of it. It was previously mentioned that you should mingle with the right crowd to learn the ropes, but don't be a follower all your life. You learn and then add your own twist to make your mark to be renowned for your uniqueness; one who can contribute to making a difference. People follow new trends, they love new ideas, so there is nothing stopping you developing your own.

Quiet or shy people could find it difficult to mingle. It's not a bad thing to be shy, but if a person feels the need to break out of their quiet nature to fit in with the rest of their counterparts, try getting professional help. There is a possibility of crawling back into their shell due to lapses in therapy sessions or lack of confidence. Although it might not be easy initially, it will get better with the right reassurance and focus. Shyness is almost impossible to overcome completely and that becomes a hindrance for your voice to be heard vehemently within a small or large group comprising girls and boys. You sometimes wonder why you cannot instantly snap out of it or why you are not as confident as some people your age. It is not your fault you are shy for that is who you are. It gets better and easier with age. Meanwhile, another way to redress this therapeutically is to start by being you; pretend to be in the midst of close family with whom you find yourself most comfortable. Try and speak a bit louder than normal and while speaking, ensure you get at least one person's attention by gesturing or get as animated as possible. That will help build your confidence with time. This is a tried and tested technique that worked for me and some of my nieces and nephews.

Girls! Michelle Obama said, *"Don't worry yourselves about men who will like or love you. You work on yourself first, become somebody in life then, you'll have them at your feet; you'll be spoilt for choice. I did not worry about who liked me and who thought I was cute when I was young. Have faith in God's plan for you and remain true to yourself"*. Today she is married to a prestigious man, a former president of the United States of America.

Ladies! Your attitude, posture and body language in public matter a great deal. Your mannerisms say a lot about you. You know it is not lady-like to yawn without covering your mouth. It doesn't speak well of you to sit with your legs apart. It is not decent for a lady to place elbows on a dining table while eating, chew with your mouth open making noises or speak with food in your mouth. Even wearing overestimated makeup will not necessarily win you extra points over other ladies where men are concerned.

A male friend once told me how he was taken by surprise when he woke up in the morning to a completely different face lying next to him. He said, *"D! My expensive white pillow slips turned brown. I was so shocked and confused I almost ran out, I thought I was in someone else's bedroom."* Simplicity is the key, ladies; going without makeup does not in any way make you less relevant. You've got to project confidence from within; trust yourself to feel good enough on the exterior. Men prefer less makeup and besides it's not all about the looks. It would be best for your man to see you bare without makeup. So when you necessarily want to look elegant or radiant with minimal amount worn, he'll appreciate the enhancement...*be prepared to finish what you started though.*

You'll be surprised how much others will learn from you; they will always want to be around and emulate you not only because of your simplicity, but also for that rare aura. Your relationship with God is what allows for this special gift. Sometimes you look in the mirror, hoping to see what it is people see that you can't – it is not your make up and not your power; it is purely God's glory radiating within you. *Simples!*

Managing finances is a vital part of your sustenance. Start putting something aside. Invest, no matter how little. When I received my first substantial salary my mother advised me to start putting some money aside for a rainy day. I thought, *Okay Mum I will.* Each time I was on the telephone to her she'd ask, *"Are you saving some money for a rainy day?"* I'd answer, *"Yes Mum."* LIE! I always tried to avoid responding to that question because I hadn't started saving. Technology hadn't progressed this far then, where I would have been inspired by various opportunities of today through social media which makes it a lot easier for us to network, market and invest. No excuse, I just wasn't saving enough and even when I did I'd always dip into it. To be honest, I rue every bit of my immature decision till this day. There's no point crying over spilt milk; learn from that and make some alterations while you still have a chance. So as a more mature parent, what I do now is put aside a certain amount from my monthly salary for various things, making it readily available for when I'll need to make payments in huge sums. It could be anything concerning car maintenance, projects, holidays or whatever I may need. Even after all relevant deductions, there'll still be a tangible amount for the odd purchases. Don't be a spendthrift take control of your finances. If you have to purchase anything luxurious do it wisely and don't make a habit of it. Trust me you'll be doing the right thing. Nowadays, there are several ways of investing or even starting a business on the side; take advantage of the system and don't get left behind.

EMOTIONS

We sometimes find ourselves becoming over-emotional in phases of our lives, especially when it comes to feeling tearful. The best way to overcome this is to let it all out when the urge for it arises. Cry without fighting back the tears; allow the tears to roll and let it take its course. Trust me you will feel a lot better and almost forget about the reason for your outburst at the time.

Never make hasty decisions when angry; you could end up regretting your actions especially if those actions were irreversible – such as retaliation due to a partner's infidelity or a trusted friend or family member's betrayal. Do not stoop to their level. When anger elapses and you feel calm what would you do if some damage was already done? *Cooked carrots cannot be reversed so be careful.* A friend once let me in on his ordeal that happened in his secondary school days. He sat his GCSCs in Science subjects, but had a very low grade in mathematics. Joshua was determined to achieve a distinction so he studied hard and was well prepared for a resit. On the day of the exam after sitting the multiple choice morning session at 9am, feeling ecstatically happy for smashing the paper he left the school premises with five class mates to go to the family house close by, to revise for the second part of the paper scheduled for 2.30pm. When it was 2.15pm they made their way back to the school premises since it was only a five-minute walk. As they turned the corner they could see students through the hall window – heads down, pens moving across sheets. They had started the second paper. They ran as fast as their legs would take them, but were stopped at the hall entrance by the principal who happened to be…*wait for it* – his paternal uncle. Unbelievably, they were kept waiting for an additional ten minutes. Imagine the adrenalin pumping at the time. When they were finally allowed in, it took Joshua minutes before he could keep his pen steady or even gather his thoughts. With all that time wasted, he was able to answer only two and a half from the five questions required. This is something Joshua had looked forward to conquering, only for his own uncle to deprive him of a distinction. After all was said and done, Joshua was given a C in mathematics. *Ouch, that did hurt!* If he had left the school on his own that morning, maybe it would have been a case of self-doubt. He would have blamed himself for getting the start time mixed up. But they were all consciously aware of a time so significant. It took Joshua years to eventually forgive his uncle. *What a life!*

A change of scenery could boost the creative mind. If ever you find yourself feeling down or alone take a walk for some fresh air; you will be amazed how refreshing that could be. You could find yourself in a whole new zone, on a different level and focused. I tell you those moments are rare, where you experience mind-blowing creativity, your own stamp; ideas pouring in like there is no tomorrow. Make sure you are out there with your writing materials because you will need them. When I am out and about or on my own in a completely different environment away from my *boudoir,* my creative side kicks in and I can tell you, I take every advantage of it. My room is where the execution takes place; I put the day's gift together and then relax.

After a moment of raised voices in your home between parents and their offspring the best way to clear the air is to allow time to do the screaming for you. Remain quiet, take deep breaths, study the ambience in the home then make your move when there is calm. What I mean by *make your move* is do something that could potentially restore friendship, peace, respect and trust. Go to the other party involved. Taking a seat beside them quietly would speak for itself. Most times people end up hugging and forgetting the whole issue began in the first place. This is the norm with some families where no love is lost, but there are others who don't know the meaning of *family*; hatred and envy oozing from every angle; siblings wishing one another an ill-fated existence. Do not give room to evil thoughts; do not let that be your family.

You feel so hurt when unappreciated by your partner. You feel stripped of every right to express yourself when at each time you pour out your heart he snaps and you always have to be the bigger person to make peace while he has his way. For the fact that you do everything possible to maintain peace is not a weakness and so should not give anyone the right to treat you with anything other than the respect and love that is required in a relationship. Even when you are being loyal and go out of your way to satisfy your partner, you are still treated with contempt. Some men sarcastically frustrate their partners especially after they've been unfaithful and even try their luck at 'gaslighting'…emotional manipulation where they deflect attention and blame to make you feel guilty. They are bent on pushing you against your principles to become equals. *Don't fall for that!* Be strong minded, stick to your beliefs and hold your head up high. The best way to get out of that kind of ugly heartache is to keep busy and believe in you. If ever your feelings towards him begin to change, make it known to him; if he truly loves you he'll do something about it. I wouldn't encourage engaging in a relationship with two men at the same time. That could easily defame or tarnish your squeaky-clean image. Men and women in a relationship ought to know that loyalty should not be taken for granted, because there might come a time when one could reach a point of no return. A woman in love will go out of her way to please her man and I believe some men do the same. *Men! If you show genuine love to your woman, you can almost certainly rest assured you'll have nothing to make your life a misery.*

This applies to both men and women and is written in the bible in the book of 1 Corinthians 7:32-35. A man is torn two ways in life whether married or not. He can devote himself to corporate works of mercy and his only worry will be to please God, while a married man has to worry about making his wife happy. In the same way, an unmarried woman can devote herself to the Lord's affairs and keep herself holy in body and spirit, while a married woman should worry about keeping her marital home safe and together. Either way, we give the Lord equal attention.

LOVE

Love is an amazing feeling. It's like air; it is invisible. It doesn't weigh on you; you cannot pin it down nor hurry it. It has a mind of its own. You can only feel it...in your heart. When you are in love you feel your heart beat irrationally at times; you become nervous when you are around your lover. Love needs love itself. It stays where it is needed, but gradually slips away if taken for granted, like a dejected child who sits in a corner isolated without friends. Even where there is conflict it remains patient; it waits peacefully and quietly to be nurtured. When that nurture isn't forthcoming it quietly slips away. Love gives its all without holding back; one heart, one love. Love cries when it hurts; it wouldn't want to do the same to the other. Love does not retaliate.

You can only love others if you love yourself. By loving yourself you're accepting who you are, inwardly and outwardly no matter how vague. You never know what others might discover within that which might seem awkward to you. People have the ability to see beyond an act. Pretending to be who you're not isn't a wise move, because it will be difficult to keep up and it will catch up with you soon enough. Some people are blessed with a special captivating aura that shines through.

You will be surprised how hugs can restore togetherness – we can also express love by supporting one another, sharing, helping, laughing together and standing as one, be it in a nuclear, compound or extended family.

Some homes are unaware of the power of love. When expressed effectively it could help improve our morale and how we relate with the outside world.

When I was in secondary school, I had the option of staying with my mum in the cantonment when she was a major in the army or the family house closer to my school. I chose the latter as it was more fun with my maternal family – grannies, uncles, aunties and cousins. Our age range was between seven and twenty. Girls outnumbered boys and every night was *suya* (grilled assorted meat) and *giggle* night. Daytime in the community was always buzzing, as there were numerous corner shops around, music blasting from our DJ next-door neighbour from morning till late over the weekends; there was never a dull moment. We never went to bed early even with school or work the next day because no one wanted to miss out on the fun around.

My grandma was a very funny woman who always joined in the fun and made us laugh. She always shouted out our names from wherever anytime she needed help with anything and could match each person to any particular job. Something amusing happened one afternoon when my nan asked my cousin in our dialect, *"I don't have to shout so loud when I need to call anyone else for help, why do I always have to shout your name severally at the top of my voice before you hear me?"* We all stopped in our tracks, gathered round; some standing akimbo while others assumed comfortable positions, waiting eagerly for that explosion of laughter. There it was; *"I think I have a bead in my ear"* said Sarah quietly.

"Bead in your ear?" my gran retorted worryingly, peering left and right at us through the top of her glasses, grimacing as if to say, *"What is she on about?"* She fought the thought of having a bead in one's ear. It was difficult to comprehend as Sarah was no three-year-old. My uncle Stan, Sarah's dad, was another hilarious person. He was summoned by his sister, my grandma. Long story short, lo and behold, there was actually a bead embedded in Sarah's ear, which was eventually taken out in the hospital. We were all relieved and happy for Sarah. A few weeks went by with little or no loud shouting from my nan. We suddenly found my uncle at the house one day; Sarah's problem had returned. This time it was my uncle who did the yelling; *"What is it you have in your ear this time – mango seed?"* We all burst out laughing. *How can that massive mango seed fit in one's ear?* we thought. He was just being his funny self. That made our day.

We had a cousin, Linda, stay with us after relocating from Ghana. She felt out of place for a while but soon realised we were all a crazy bunch. Linda and I soon became close enough that we helped one another with our individual chores. We took turns styling our hair every Sunday afternoon ready for school. She was better than me in the hair department, so my hair was always looking neater and nicer. There were times when her dad would come to visit her with little or no pocket money for her to last the month. Meanwhile I had monthly pocket money separately from my mum and dad to last forever; I could afford anything reasonable a teenager wanted. So I decided sharing would make her a lot happier and focused.

I was only two years older, but took her as my kid sister. I wanted the best for her in grades and everything else. We became inseparable, supported and encouraged one another. She went on to study nursing and midwifery. She is now married to a doctor with two beautiful children. It all worked out.

On my way to work on the Jubilee Line Underground Tube Service one morning to start a 9am shift, I noticed an elderly Sudanese man standing; both hands were wrapped round the pole in the middle section of the train to steady him. An arm kept going round his back, as if to say, *it will be alright, we'll soon get there.* Anyone could tell that the arm was his son's. He must have been in his mid-forties and there was a striking resemblance. He kept whispering into his dad's ear and dad kept nodding, his eyes fixated with pride; his own son – showing so much love and care. They got off the train three stops after. I was filled with emotion and in awe of what I had witnessed. It felt like I was watching a well packaged five-minute movie. The son was so protective of his dad. He must have inspired his son in so many ways and now, we see a reflection of reciprocated love and care.

An Asian friend who lives with his wife, two daughters and son (now married) once told me how he thought it necessary to address corrective measures to his son's wife, with regards to expressing love in the family whenever they came visiting. Each time she wanted to leave a room full of people, at bedtime, she would just murmur *"Goodnight"* under her breath without paying any attention to others or keeping an eye contact, not even with her own husband. This had gone on long enough for her father-in-law to nip in the bud – he took out time to enlighten her. It happened that she was not quite used to hugging or kissing goodnight because it was hardly done in her own family home. After a while, she began putting in the effort; *there was a result!* She became happier and at ease with everyone; love blossomed!

I went further to meet with a female colleague, Sonia, who happens to be a single parent, to discern the true nature of parenthood. I wanted to know how close she was with her daughter, Emily. Sonia has a good relationship with her daughter, but it could become strenuous at times. She recalls the transition period from nursery to primary education which was a bit stressful, having to run affairs alone. Sonia has had the opportunity to view things differently now, being closer to God. According to her, God has opened her eyes to a lot of things for strength which sees her through daily challenges. She makes it a priority to strike that balance between her life growing up and Emily's, as it was a completely different era years back growing up when children and parents could hardly be seen sharing jokes freely or permitted more space than required. Mother and daughter both enjoy each other's company and are determined to maintain that closeness without giving room to any pessimistic outlook on life. Sonia would do whatever it took to reverse that negative sense of approach. She believes the more open parents are with their child/children, the easier it will be for the kids to discuss any underlying issues. That rings a bell!

When you fight for something with love in your heart, love will definitely surmount any piercing difficulty.

The best love of all is God's immeasurable love for us. He loves us unconditionally and no human can compete with that. God has a sweet, pure and sacred heart and we can only but pray for a piece of His kind of love.

CONCLUSION

Finding Yourself! In this day and age, we are privileged to have help at our finger tips. Thanks to various professional methods available: the internet, social media or face-to-face. We are allowed to show emotion without the need to bottle them all up. There are still a number of people in our community who experience difficulties, such as personal, relationship or financial issues which are crucial to our health, but choose to remain silent rather than ask for help.

Patience is the key to success in all endeavours.

Each and every one has a gift; let us reach out and show love to one another. I promise you! Love will make you feel fulfilled and at peace.

REFLECTION -The apple does not fall far from the tree. My daughter reflects my personality in many ways, as she re-lives/emulates almost every stage when I was her age. It continues to reflect my personal thoughts on my childhood, the family house in which I grew up and other families around in the same community. Every positive feedback about our children gives us great pride as parents, knowing we have done right by them only by the special grace of God. While putting these notes together, God was in control. I felt connected and filled with the Holy Spirit. I can confidently tell that right from the beginning, as far back as the idea of composing this book, it has been God's will.

The tunnel does not have to be dark...you are your thoughts; constitute positive thoughts in your mind. You can have light in and at the end of the tunnel...it does not have to be dark.

You hold your own light in your hands.

APPRECIATION

All glory, honour and praise to my heavenly Father who made it possible for me to express and share my faith and trust in Him with others, so they may understand and believe that our Lord always keeps his word. I thank everyone who spared their precious time for interviews and to the priests who accurately confirmed the religious sections; may God bless you all. A big shout out to my dearest loving daughter, Monica Tori Olaitan Alero Ojewale, to whom I dedicate this book. She was always patient and interested in listening to my lengthy unscheduled talks. May God show her goodness and mercy, grant her wisdom, knowledge, understanding, counsel, fortitude, piety and fear of the Lord; the gifts of the Holy Spirit...Amen

REFERENCES

Denzel Washington (extracts from quotes)

Imbumba Yamadoda (Inspirational Blogger)

Michelle Obama (extracts from quotes)

The Holy Bible

www.skillsyouneed.com

WRITER

My name is Doreen Esijeminé Aderonké Omaghomi, born in Stockport, Manchester England on 5th August, to Nigerian parents; Late Prince Dayspring Uwalogho Omaghomi and Late Major Clara Bolajoko Omaghomi. I am an Itsekiri woman, from Bateren village, Warri, Delta state; the mid-western part of Nigeria.

I stand as the intermediary between my generation and the next, our children, to inform, share and explain what some of our parents inadvertently failed to share with us.

This book would have been titled "TUNNEL THOUGHTS", due to the fact that I started writing while employed as a Train Operator. It is not suitable on this occasion for people to associate tunnels and darkness with this book, so I decided against that title. There were many other titles before settling for INSPIRATIONAL VALUES.

One thing I am sure of is that I was influenced by the Holy Spirit to share these experiences.

GOD IS LOVE.

Thank you all for your time.

 ™ DarfourChapters ©

Dafour Design Concepts Ltd

Email: dafourchapters@gmail.com

 @dafourchapters

 @dafour5chapters

 Doreen Omaghomi

Ingram Content Group UK Ltd.
Milton Keynes UK
UKHW010805190623
423681UK00015B/655